914.47

This book is to be returned on or before
the last date stamped below.

-7. MAR. ...

FLINT, D.
The Baltic States   914.47

PERSHORE HIGH SCHOOL
LIBRARY

18340   LIBREX

THE FORMER SOVIET STATES

THE BALTIC STATES
ESTONIA • LATVIA LITHUANIA

By
David C. Flint

FRANKLIN WATTS
London: New York: Toronto: Sydney

© Aladdin Books Ltd 1992

All rights reserved

Printed in Belguim

Designed and produced by
Aladdin Books Ltd
28 Percy Street
London W1P 9FF

First published
in Great Britain in 1992 by
Franklin Watts Ltd.
96 Leonard Street
London EC2A 4RH

ISBN 0 7496 1061 1

A CIP catalogue record for this book is available from the British Library.

The consultant is Dr. John Channon of the School
of Slavonic and Eastern European Studies, London, UK.

Series Design:	David West
Designer:	Rob Hillier
Editor:	Catherine Bradley
Picture Research:	Emma Krikler

CONTENTS

INTRODUCTION	4
UNITED BUT SEPARATE	6
PEOPLE AND PLACES	8
TRADE AND EMPIRE	10
INDEPENDENT LITHUANIA	12
UNDER THE TSARS	14
BALTIC AWAKENING	16
SOVIET WINTER	18
THE ROAD TO FREEDOM	20
THE FINAL PUSH	22
THE POLITICAL OUTLOOK	24
THE ECONOMIC FUTURE	26
FACTS AND FIGURES	28
CHRONOLOGY AND FAMOUS PEOPLE	30
INDEX	32

INTRODUCTION

The three newly independent Baltic states of Estonia, Latvia, and Lithuania appear as though they are in a corner of northern Europe, on the southeastern coast of the Baltic Sea. In fact, geographically they are at the heart of Europe, whose centre is in eastern Lithuania, 25 kilometres (15 miles) north of the country's capital, Vilnius.

The Baltic states lie at the meeting point of Eastern and Western Europe and act as an economic and cultural link between Russia and the West. Since the Middle Ages, rival parties have fought over the Baltic lands, to control the ports and trade routes of the Baltic Sea. The Baltic peoples have had many rulers, but their sense of nationhood is strong.

In 1991, the Baltic states played a central role in the break-up of the Soviet Union. Eleven of the former Soviet states joined the Commonwealth of Independent States (C.I.S.). However, the Baltic states chose not to, and now face an uncertain future.

UNITED BUT SEPARATE

"A chain of life binds us together," declared President Vytautas Landsbergis of Lithuania, addressing the Latvian parliament in 1990 before it voted to restore Latvian independence. However, while the Baltic states are tied together by geography and a shared history, particularly in the twentieth century when they endured nearly 50 years of communist rule, they are very different.

Lithuania is a Catholic country as a result of its historic ties with Poland, while for centuries Baltic German nobles ruled Estonia and Latvia, and these are now Protestant countries. Traditionally Lithuania has been less industrialised and more agricultural than the other two Baltic states.

Under Soviet rule a massive industrialisation programme in Latvia was accompanied by large-scale Russian immigration. This almost made Latvians a minority in their own country – making up barely 50 per cent of the population. Lithuania was largely spared this problem, and today Lithuanians make up 80 per cent of the country's population, although fewer than half the total population of its capital, Vilnius, are native Lithuanians.

The ancient city of Riga, capital of Latvia.

The economy

Economically, the Baltic states are not too small to survive. However, their economies have been severely disrupted by the break-up of the Soviet Union, which had previously provided heavily

In August 1989 the Baltic peoples formed a human chain from Estonia, through Latvia, to Lithuania.

Communism and the market

After 1945, the three Baltic states were forced to change their economies and become communist. This meant that land and industry could not belong to private individuals, but belonged to the state.

All decisions about the economy were made by communist officials in Moscow, the capital of the Soviet Union. The Soviet Union decided where to build new factories and power plants, and how much they should produce, what prices they should charge, and how much people should be paid.

In fact, under the communist system, people in the Baltic states were considerably better off than people in the other Soviet republics. However, they were not as well off as those in Western Europe, which did not have a communist system.

With the break-up of the Soviet Union, the Baltic states must reorganise their economies. Businesses and commerce must return to private hands. Food and goods will have to be sold at home and abroad on the open market.

subsidised supplies of raw materials as well as guaranteed markets for the goods manufactured in the Baltic states. Also, after 50 years of Soviet industrialisation, the Baltic states have much industrial pollution to clean up. The cost of repairing the damage and reorganising their factories and farms to cope with the new economic situation will be extremely high.

The Baltic states have nevertheless begun their new independent lives with some advantages over the other former Soviet republics. They have a skilled work force with expertise in modern technologies – fostered during the years when the Baltic states were used as an economic and industrial laboratory by the Soviet Union. They are also knowledgeable in the area of banking. Many of the Baltic states' farms are in private hands and can readily adapt to the demands of free enterprise.

The Baltic Sea is famous for its fish.

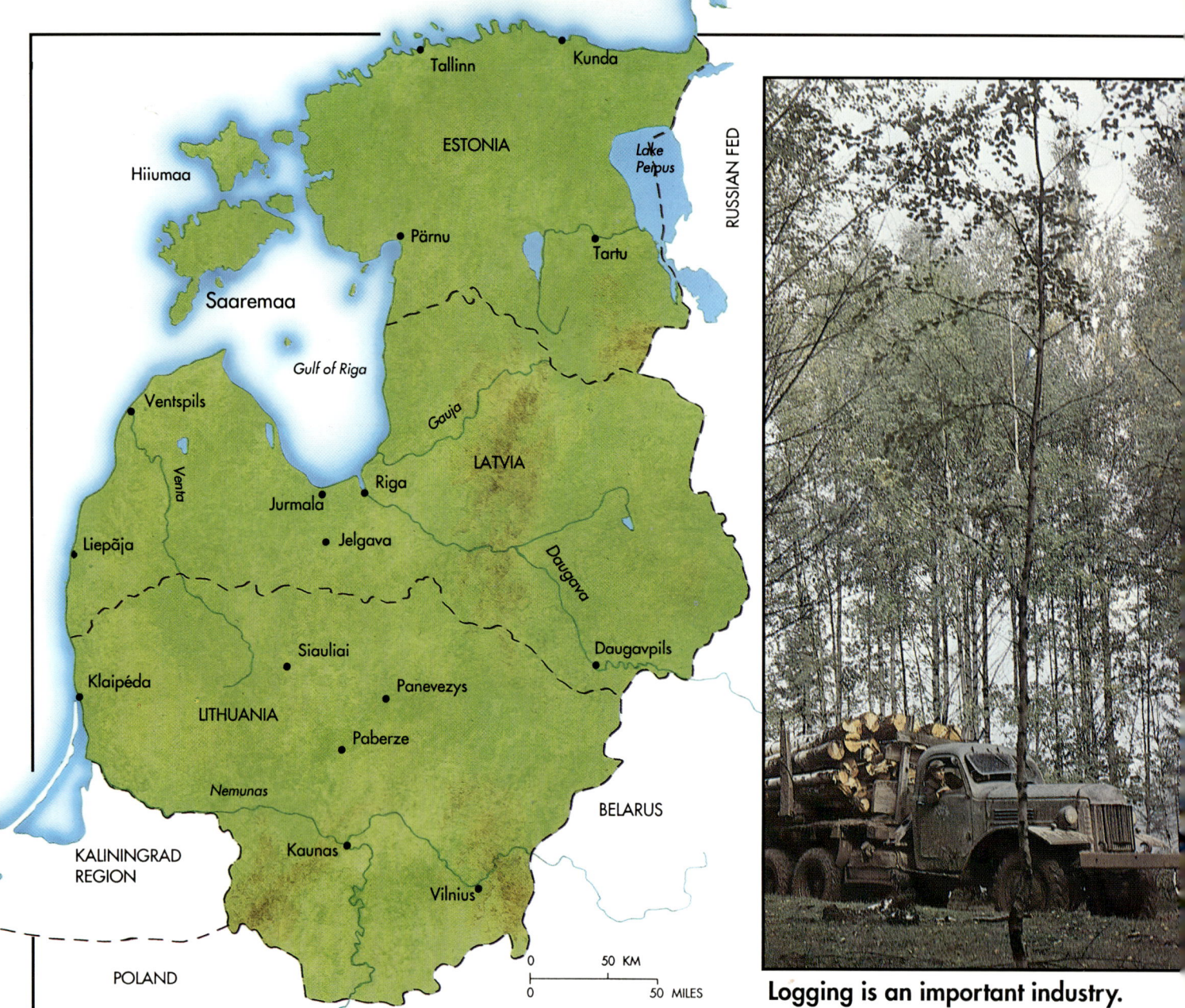

Logging is an important industry.

PEOPLE AND PLACES

The Baltic states cover an area roughly the size of Washington State in America. They form part of the large coastal plain of northern Europe, and are separated from Scandinavia by the narrow strip of the Baltic Sea and its gulfs.

In the north of the Baltic lands, off the coast of Estonia, there is an archipelago, just as there is in the Scandinavian peninsula, and southern Finland. Lithuania and Latvia are dotted with many thousands of lakes in a wooded landscape resembling that of Sweden and Finland.

Estonia contains the Baltic states' most important mineral resource, the oil-shale deposits located in the north-east of the country. The absence of coal and oil in the Baltic states has made oil-shale a key fuel source. About 15 per cent of the mainland of Estonia is covered with peat bogs, which provide a useful local fuel.

8

This oil-shale power station in north-east Estonia used to produce power for the Soviet Union.

The people
The combined population of the Baltic states is 8 million. The great majority of the Baltic people live in cities – 72 per cent of the population of Estonia, 72 per cent of the population of Latvia, and 65 per cent of the population of Lithuania.

Lithuanians and Latvians are Balts and can understand each other's native tongues at a basic level. Neither can communicate with Estonians, whose language is closely related to Finnish. On the other hand, Estonians can understand Finnish television programmes.

The Russian minority
At present, almost 2.8 million people of non-Baltic origin, 80 per cent of them Russian, live in the Baltic states. In north-east Estonia, there are areas where Russians make up 90 per cent of the population. Although many of them wish to become citizens of the Baltic states, large numbers do not speak the Baltic languages and continue to live in Russian-only areas, where they have little contact with the local people.

Many Russians were opposed to the fight for independence in 1988-91. Those who wish to become citizens of the Baltic states will be required to pass a citizen's test. The large Russian minorities may find themselves without the right to vote if they fail the citizen's test. This could lead to unrest.

Pollution
Pollution is particularly severe in north-east Estonia, near Kohtla-Jarve, centre of the country's oil-shale industry. The land, waterways, and the Baltic Sea have suffered from the wasteful burning of oil-shale as an energy source for St. Petersburg (formerly Leningrad).

There are many thousands of rivers in the Baltic states, but these have been heavily polluted by industrial waste and chemical fertilizers, herbicides, and pesticides used in agriculture. The coastal waters off Estonia and Latvia are also heavily polluted by industrial waste.

The Baltic states have lodged claims running into billions of dollars for pollution damage, some of it caused by the Soviet armed forces. However, there is little or no chance that the successors of the Soviet Union, the C.I.S., will pay any compensation. They have enough economic problems of their own.

TRADE AND EMPIRE

The native populations of the Baltic states are descended from the people who settled on eastern shores of the Baltic Sea about 4,000 years ago. There were two groups, one speaking Finnish and the other Baltic languages. In the north were Finnic tribes. One, the Livs gave their name to the medieval province of Livonia. In the south lived the ancestors of the Latvians and Lithuanians.

From the second to the fifth centuries A.D. the Baltic tribes enjoyed a golden age, in which they developed a trading empire based on metalwork, which covered north-eastern Europe. Around A.D. 650, Vikings from Scandinavia began to launch attacks on the prosperous coastal regions of the Baltic. For the next 600 years the Balts and the Vikings alternately fought and traded with each other.

Tacitus

At the end of the first century A.D., the Roman historian Tacitus wrote a history of Germany. He described the people living on the Baltic Sea. They were called the Aestii, and they traded in amber (a trade which has continued to the present day).

He also mentioned that they were able farmers, and that in the growing of maize and other crops they worked "with more patience than is customary among the lazy Germans". It was the Aestii who probably gave their name to Estonia.

Christian conquerors

The homelands of the Baltic peoples were medieval Europe's last pagan stronghold. In the

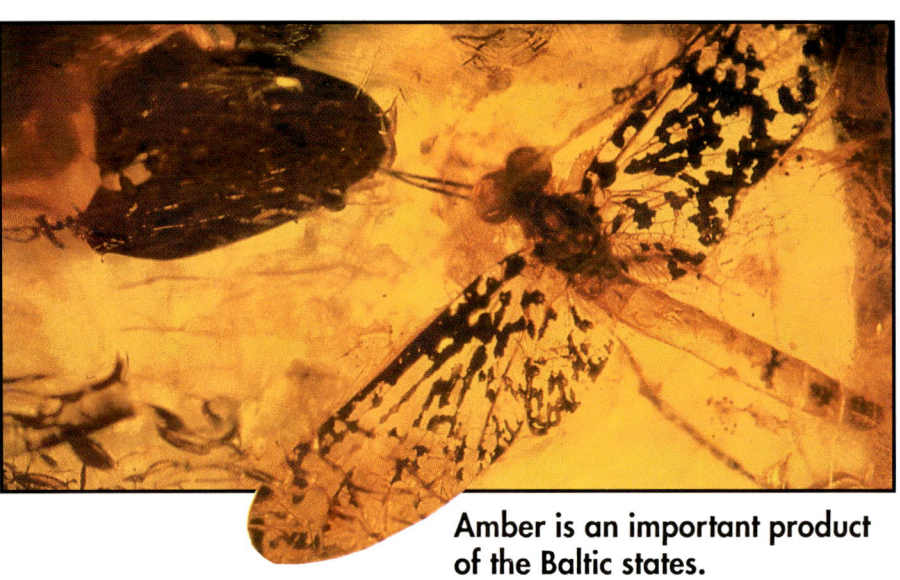

Amber is an important product of the Baltic states.

10

twelfth century, Christianity was forcibly introduced to Latvia and Estonia, a brutal process which lasted 100 years. Trade followed the establishment of the church.

The Danish kings ruled northern Estonia, where the port of Tallinn was an important trading post between Russia and the rest of Europe. Here, furs, wax, and slaves from Russia were exchanged for salt, textiles, and weapons.

German influence

German merchants colonised the banks of the Dvina River, which was also important for trade. At the mouth of the Dvina they established the city of Riga.

A military order, the German Brothers of the Sword, was sent on a crusade to conquer the outlying countryside. The invaders colonised, baptised, and enslaved the local people. In 1346 the Danes sold their lands in Estonia and Livonia (made up of southern Estonia and eastern Latvia) to another military order, the Teutonic Knights.

In 1561 the Teutonic Knights were disbanded and there followed centuries of war.

Swedish wars

Sweden gained part of northern Latvia and Estonia, which became Swedish territory in 1629, and fought the Russians for control of Livonia. The Baltic people suffered death and famine, and by the middle of the seventeenth century Estonia's pre-war population of 280,000 had fallen to barely 100,000.

Russian power

The next major upheaval in the region came with a renewed drive by Russia to establish itself on the Baltic coastline. In 1721 Russia gained possession of Livonia and Estland (northern Estonia).

The Baltic-German nobles and merchants, who had ruled the region since the Middle Ages, were able to retain their privileges. They eventually became loyal subjects of the Russian empire.

Teutonic Knights of the fourteenth century

INDEPENDENT LITHUANIA

In the Middle Ages Lithuania was an independent state, which in its heyday was the most powerful in central Europe. Protected by lakes and impenetrable forests, its pagan people were able to resist the Christian crusaders. Then, under the leadership of Mindaugas, the Baltic tribes in Lithuania and parts of Belarus became a kingdom.

In 1237, Mindaugas defeated the Brothers of the Sword. Shortly afterwards, Mindaugas converted to Christianity, but his subjects remained stubbornly pagan. Mindaugas was assassinated in 1263, but the state he had created survived his death. In the hands of his successors, Lithuania managed not only to contain the attacks of the Teutonic Knights but also to expand eastwards.

The last pagans in Europe entered Christendom on their own terms. In 1386 the Lithuanian prince, Jagiello, became king of Poland by marrying the Polish queen, Jadwiga, and ordered the mass baptism of his subjects. Under the rule of Vytautas the Great (1410-1430), Lithuania stretched from the gates of Moscow to the shores of the Black Sea.

Union with Poland

In 1410, the Lithuanians and their Polish allies decisively defeated the Teutonic Knights at Tannenberg. Thereafter, the fortunes of Poland and Lithuania rose and fell

The Lithuanian attack on Moscow

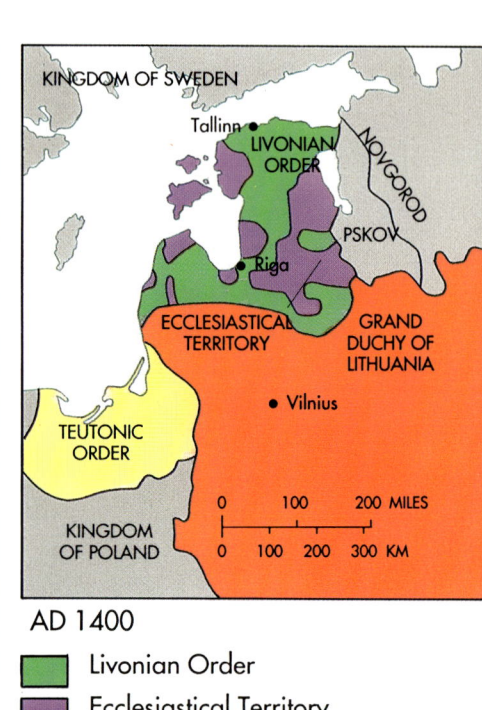

AD 1400

- Livonian Order
- Ecclesiastical Territory
- Grand Duchy of Lithuania
- Teutonic Order

1569

- Estland
- Polish Lithuanian Commonwealth
- Prussia

together. The union between the countries was formalised in 1569, and lasted until the end of the eighteenth century.

Gradually Lithuania became the junior partner. Its people maintained the Catholic religion, and its nobles spoke Polish. So, in Lithuania, Latvia, and Estonia the rulers spoke a different language from the peasants.

As the Swedes took over Estonia and clashed with Russia over Livonia, the Lithuanians and the Poles seized southern Livonia. In the seventeenth century, the eastern part of Livonia became Lithuanian.

Russian control

By the eighteenth century, however, the Polish-Lithuanian alliance was being menaced by powerful neighbours – Prussia, Russia, and Austria. In 1795 the Lithuanian territories became part of the Russian Empire, which was ruled by the Tsar (Russian for king).

A fourteenth-century castle in Lithuania

The Teutonic Knights
The Teutonic Knights were one of several groups of crusading knights who, in the 12th century, organised themselves into military orders to protect Christian pilgrims in the Holy Land. The soldier-monks of the Teutonic Order were Germans, and in 1225 Duke Conrad of Masovia invited them to conquer the last pagan tribes in Europe, the Prussians and Lithuanians.

They were successful in Prussia, transforming a wilderness into a wealthy state. In the Baltics, however, they suffered a crushing defeat at Tannenberg in 1410, and in 1466 were forced to acknowledge the king of Poland as their feudal overlord.

By the sixteenth century, the order's fighting days were over. During this time of religious upheaval, known as the Reformation, the Teutonic Knights became Protestants. In 1618, what remained of their lands passed on to a German prince.

Russian rule in Lithuania led to the persecution of the Jews. Here Jewish people are expelled in 1844.

UNDER THE TSARS

As part of the Tsarist Empire, the Lithuanians remained separate from the Latvians and Estonians. They kept their Catholic faith and were ruled by Polish-speaking nobles. German gentry and merchants ruled the remaining Baltic provinces. Lithuania was still an agricultural backwater, while Estonia and Latvia became centres of Russian trade and industry. As more and more factories were built, peasants moved to the cities. By the end of the nineteenth century, Riga had become the sixth largest city in the Russian empire, with a population of some 250,000, mainly Germans, Russians, Latvians and Jews.

In the second half of the nineteenth century, the Russians tried to make the Baltic provinces more Russian – Russification. Lithuanians had to convert to the Russian Orthodox faith. A similar attack was made on the Protestants in Latvia and Estonia. In 1885, Russian became the language of the educational system and the government. In Lithuania, the nobles' estates were confiscated and divided among the peasants, because the nobles had sided with the Poles when they rebelled against the Tsar in 1830 and 1868.

Revolutionary unrest

By the beginning of the twentieth century the Baltic people had had enough of Russian rule. The revolutionary unrest in Russia of 1905 spread to the Baltic provinces. In Latvia and Estonia, the people attacked the Baltic Germans. Many of them decided to emigrate to the German Empire.

After the 1905 Revolution, the Tsarist regime made some concessions in the Baltic provinces. The people were allowed to use the Estonian, Latvian and Lithuanian languages. But the Baltic people's demands for self-government were ignored.

Russian collapse

In 1914 the Russian Empire became involved in a war against Germany and Austria-Hungary. The strains of fighting World War I, threatened the Tsar's rule. By 1915, all of Lithuania, and parts of Latvia had been occupied by the German army. The Russian war effort collapsed in 1917, and by the beginning of 1918, the Germans controlled the rest of Latvia and Estonia. The days of Russian rule of the Baltic provinces were over.

Nationalism and language

The Russification policy in the second half of the nineteenth century could not stop the Baltic people's desire to have their own nations. In Latvia and Estonia in particular, there was a growing educated middle class, who knew that throughout Europe people were trying to establish their own nations. The growing nationalism was expressed in a renewed interest in the native languages and folklore. This took on great political importance in Latvia and Estonia, which, unlike Lithuania, had no history as independent states.

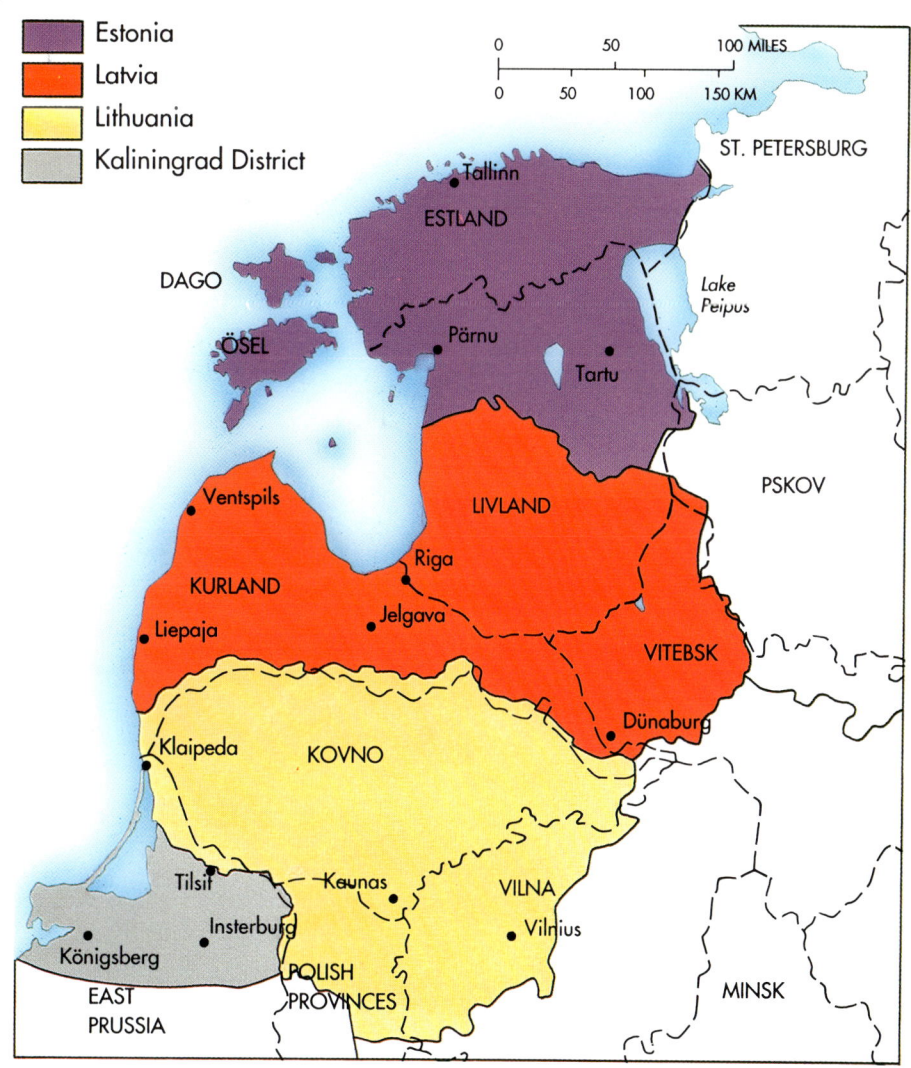

15

BALTIC AWAKENING

A demonstration in Riga, Latvia, in 1919

The collapse of the Russian Empire in 1917, and the defeat of Germany in 1918, allowed the Baltic peoples to set up their own nation states. Estonia declared its independence on 24 February, 1918, and in the autumn of that year successfully fought off an attack by the Red Army, the Russian communist force. Lithuania had declared its independence on 16 February, 1918. By the summer of 1919, it had gained control of its territory, but was forced to leave its capital, Vilnius, in Polish hands.

Latvian independence

In Latvia, when independence was declared on 18 November, 1918, there was a complicated struggle between local communists and German soldiers. The German and communist threats were overcome, and by 1920 Latvia was independent. That year, the three Baltic nations made separate peace treaties with the new communist Russian Empire, the Soviet Union.

Peace and prosperity

Lithuania, Latvia, and Estonia became parliamentary democracies. This meant that every few years the people had to vote for representatives to form a new government. They faced the difficult task of rebuilding their countries as many factories and farms had been destroyed during the years of fighting. To make sure there was both political stability and economic progress, each of the Baltic states launched a programme of land reform. In the years 1918-39, the Baltic states grew

The signing of the Nazi-Soviet pact in 1939.

16

A demonstration in Tallinn, Estonia, after the Soviet invasion of August 1940.

prosperous by exporting meat, poultry and dairy products to Western Europe. Industry also recovered, but democracy failed. In 1926, a military coup in Lithuania brought a dictator, Antonas Smetona, to power. In March 1934, in Estonia, one party seized power, and a few days later the same happened in Latvia.

Outside threats

Soon the Baltic states came under threat from their powerful neighbours, Germany and the Soviet Union. In September 1939, a secret agreement was made between the two countries – it became known as the Nazi-Soviet Pact – in which Germany agreed that the Soviet Union could take over Estonia, Latvia and Lithuania.

On September 1, 1939, Germany invaded Poland, and World War II began. The Baltic states were squeezed between two hostile powers with no allies to help them. In June 1940, as the German army overran France, the Red Army occupied the Baltic states. They offered no resistance and became part of the Soviet Union.

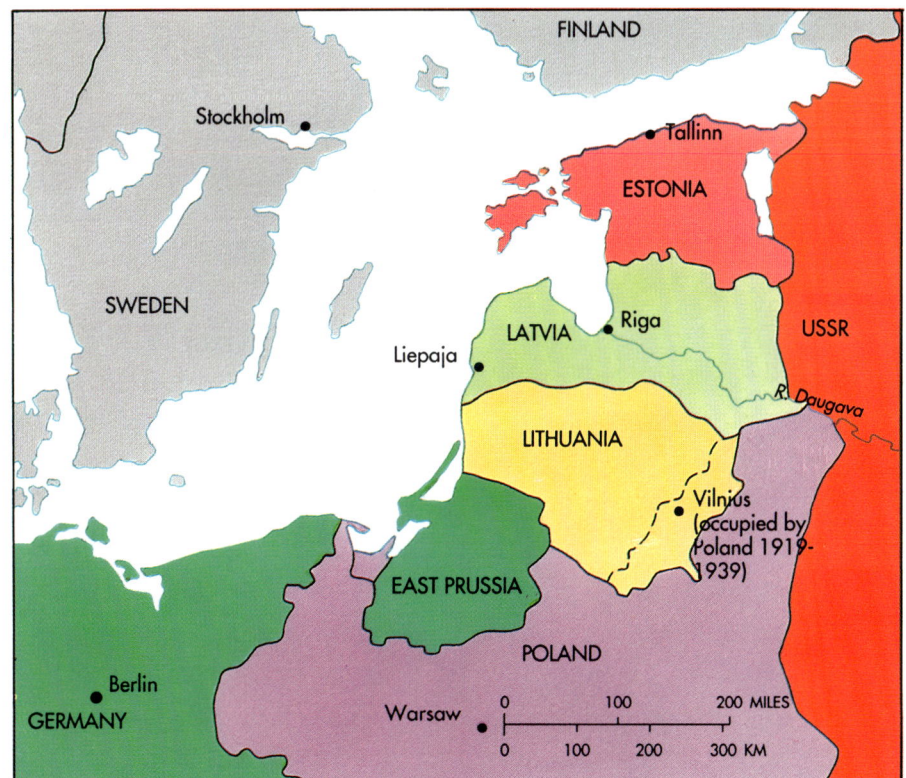

THE BALTICS, 1938

A banner proclaims "Long live Soviet Latvia".

SOVIET WINTER

The Soviet occupation of the Baltic states ended in the summer of 1941. Germany invaded the Soviet Union and quickly overran Lithuania, Latvia and Estonia. Thousands of Balts rose up against the Red Army as it was driven out by the Germans, but Germany had no intention of restoring independence to the Baltic states. They became little more than German colonies, and were ruthlessly exploited to produce food and goods for Germany.

The Nazis, who ruled the German Reich, wanted to kill all the Jews in their territories. Lithuania had the largest Jewish population – in June 1941 it stood at some 250,000. By the summer of 1944, 90 per cent of them had died in Nazi concentration camps.

Soviet rule

In July 1944, Germany was losing the war, and the Red Army overran the Baltic states. Lithuania, Latvia and Estonia again came under Soviet rule. The Baltic people felt this was no different than the Nazi occupation, and resistance groups, known as the Forest Brothers, remained active in all three countries until the early 1950s.

In the 1950s, the outside world knew nothing of these events in the Baltic

Soviet troops cross a river as they approach Riga in 1944.

republics. All contact with the West was forbidden. Foreign journalists were banned, and it was not until the 1960s that a few tourists were allowed into the republics.

Meanwhile, the Soviet Union set about changing the Baltic republics' economies. Agriculture, previously in private hands, was brought under state control, and thousands of peasants were sent to Siberia. This had a catastrophic effect on farming. Agricultural output dropped, and only returned to 1939 levels in the mid-1960s. It has been estimated that between 1944 and 1955 as many as 500,000 people were deported from the Baltic republics.

After the war, the Soviet leaders launched an industrialisation and urbanisation programme in Latvia and Estonia, and to a lesser extent in Lithuania. Many workers from other parts of the Soviet Union came to live in Estonia and Latvia as a result of this policy. By 1980, the Latvians were in danger of becoming a minority in their own country.

Internal problems

Industrialisation brought other problems. There was a severe housing shortage because Russian immigrants got housing before the local populations. Russian was enforced as the language of the workplace, even where the immigrants were in a minority.

For security reasons, the Baltic peoples were generally excluded from jobs in shipping, fishing and air transport. Estonia and Latvia also suffered huge environmental damage. The landscape was disfigured by huge, outdated factories and smokestacks.

A nuclear power plant in Lithuania. Many of these Soviet-built plants are out-of-date and unsafe.

A pro-independence meeting in Tallinn, Estonia, in December 1988

THE ROAD TO FREEDOM

In the early 1980s, a visitor to the historic cities of Tallinn or Riga, respectively the capitals of Estonia and Latvia, would have been struck by the contrast these cities presented with the rest of the Soviet Union. Their citizens were far better dressed than elsewhere in the Soviet Union, met to drink in charming, seemingly well-stocked cafés, and listened to the latest Western pop music. Soviet filmmakers regularly used these cities as stand-ins for real Western locations.

Baltic resentment
This was of little comfort to the Baltic peoples. They knew how much more prosperous were their Scandinavian neighbours. Latvia produced most of the Soviet Union's radios, refrigerators, washing machines and other goods – but there always seemed to be a shortage of them at home. They also resented the Russian immigrants, many of whom did not even bother to learn their language.

In the 1970s, there had been some protests

Gorbachev

In 1985, Mikhail Sergeyevich Gorbachev became the most powerful man in the Soviet Union when he became general secretary of the Communist Party. He was much younger than previous leaders and immediately talked about reforming communism. He also promised to end the Cold War between East and West.

Gorbachev gained much praise from the leaders of the United States, Western Europe, and other countries. However, at home he became increasingly unpopular as his reforms did not appear to improve the economic situation.

In January 1990, Gorbachev visited Lithuania in an attempt to prevent the break-up of the Soviet Union, of which he was now president. In August 1991, he survived a coup launched against him by hardline communist leaders who did not want to reform the communist system. He was soon eclipsed by his old rival Boris Yeltsin, the President of Russia. Gorbachev resigned in December 1991. He had fought valiantly to save the Soviet Union, but it had been a lost cause.

Mikhail Gorbachev and Boris Yeltsin

against Soviet rule. In 1972, a Lithuanian, Romas Kalanta, burned himself to death in a public park. Protest also found an outlet in the huge open-air song festivals in the Baltic republics, notably in Estonia. In the mid-1980s, concern over industrial pollution prompted a series of mass demonstrations.

The Popular Fronts

In 1985, Mikhail Gorbachev came to power in the Soviet Union, determined to reform communism by introducing *perestroika* (restructuring) and *glasnost* (openness). These reforms were supposed to keep the Soviet Union intact, but they soon led to its destruction. In the Baltic republics the openness allowed new nationalist movements, known as the Popular Fronts, to spring up in 1988. They were broad-based movements and included communists. They demanded first self-government, and then, as the pace of events accelerated, full independence for the Baltic republics.

21

THE FINAL PUSH

Initially the pace was set by Lithuania, which had fewer Russian immigrants (80 per cent of the republic's total population were Lithuanians). Both Latvia and Estonia had large Russian minorities, many of whom were deeply hostile to Baltic independence.

In May 1989, Lithuania's parliament, formerly an unimportant body that did what the Soviet rulers told it to do, committed itself to full independence. Lithuanian was restored as the official language, and freedom of religion and the press were introduced. Similar measures were passed in the Latvian and Estonian parliaments.

On 23 August, 1989, the Baltic peoples marked the fiftieth anniversary of the Nazi-Soviet pact by forming a human chain stretching across the three republics. In February 1990, the pro-independence Popular Front, known as "Sajudis", won over 90 per cent of the seats in the parliamentary elections in Lithuania.

January 1991: Soviet paratroopers attack the crowd in Vilnius.

Nationalists take to the streets of Estonia, carrying their country's flag, in February 1989.

Full independence

On 11 March, Lithuania made the decisive break with the Soviet Union, and passed a law which restored Lithuania's independence as a nation. Outside the parliament building, crowds tore down the hammer and sickle – symbol of the Soviet Union.

In Latvia and Estonia, the Popular Fronts won 74 per cent and 78 per cent of a vote on full independence. This was remarkable considering that these republics had so many non-natives living in them – 49 per cent in Latvia and 38.5 per cent in Estonia. These moves received no support from Western governments, which were still trying to ensure that Gorbachev remained in power and the Soviet Union remained intact.

In April 1990, the Soviet Union responded to the developments in Lithuania by cutting off all supplies of oil, medical items, and other essential goods. The Lithuanians were forced to back down. On 29 June, the Lithuanian parliament agreed to freeze independence for 100 days while talks continued with the Soviet leaders.

A violent response

Having wielded an economic weapon, the Soviet Union then resorted to violence. In January 1991, airborne troops were sent in to crush the independence movements in the Baltic republics. In Vilnius on 11 January, they killed 15 civilians, part of a human shield of 10,000 people surrounding the Lithuanian parliament. On 20 January, Soviet interior ministry forces killed five Latvians as they stormed a government building in Riga.

Foreign correspondents and television crews covered events and the Soviets had to back down. Then, in August 1991, Soviet conservatives tried to overthrow Gorbachev. This failed, and in its wake, in September 1991, Lithuania, Latvia and Estonia demanded and received from the rapidly disintegrating Soviet Union, recognition of their independence.

The Lithuanian parliament voted to restore independence in 1990.

23

THE POLITICAL OUTLOOK

The Baltic states face a host of political and economic problems, which cast a cloud over their political future. The issue of citizenship – and the future of Russian and other minorities – remains at the top of the political agenda. Political stability may come with economic progress, but currently everyone is suffering from economic chaos. Even the most important politicians can be affected. In February 1992, the Lithuanian prime minister, Gediminas Vagnorius, complained that he was one of many state officials who had not been paid his salary.

A year earlier in Lithuania, in February 1991, price increases of 300 percent sparked violent protests which led to their cancellation and the resignation of the government. In Estonia, where industrial production fell by one third between January 1991 and February 1992, and fuel prices increased tenfold, the economic crisis forced the resignation of prime minister Edgar Savissar, who had declared a state of emergency.

Soviet troop withdrawals

Most of these problems result from the collapse of the Soviet Union. Another problem is the presence of Soviet troops – about 150,000 – in the Baltic states. About half of them are stationed in Lithuania. The Russian Federation is responsible for these troops but negotiations about their withdrawal have been long and difficult. Russia says the troops cannot be withdrawn until there is enough housing for them at home. The Baltic governments, however, see the troops as a threat to their stability. They fear that fighting will break out between the troops and local civilians. There is also the possibility that a different government in Russia might use these troops to win back the Baltic states. The first troop withdrawals began in Lithuania in February, 1992.

Fuel shortages are becoming more common.

Relations with the outside world

Following recognition of their independence by the Soviet Union, the Baltic states joined the United Nations and other international agencies. Their sports teams will be able to compete internationally under their own flags and did so in the recent Olympics.

It will be some time, however, before the Baltic states can take part fully in the economic and political life of Western Europe. They will not be able to join the European Community (E.C.) for at least 10 years. In the meantime, it is difficult for the Baltic states to export their agricultural produce to Western Europe because of the E.C.'s policies.

The Baltic states are looking to develop close economic partnerships with their Scandinavian neighbors. Together they will form a Baltic trading bloc. The Baltic states also need to develop good relations with Germany. At present, however, Germany is having to pay for the costs of reuniting with the former communist country of East Germany. It can offer only limited help to its neighbors. When this problem is overcome, and when the newly independent republics of the former Soviet Union emerge from the current economic chaos, the Baltic states will resume their historic role as the link between East and West.

The first former Soviet troops leave Vilnius in Lithuania in February 1992.

THE ECONOMIC FUTURE

In the short term the economic outlook is discouraging. The Baltic states still use the rouble as their currency. The rouble is worthless outside the former Soviet Union, and virtually worthless inside it. An unstable currency means that prices can rise very quickly. Each of the Baltic states wants to introduce its own currency, but this will have to be done very carefully to stop black marketeers from making a quick profit. At present, using Western currency – particularly U.S. dollars – is the only reliable way of doing business in the Baltic states.

Energy needs

Apart from peat and oil-shale, the Baltic states have no energy resources of their own. Traditionally they imported petrol and gas from the Soviet Union at heavily subsidised prices. Now they must pay world prices for fuel. Another problem is that supplies from the former Soviet Union are becoming increasingly unreliable. As a result, the cost of energy has soared. In Lithuania, which is heavily dependent on energy from Belarus, fuel prices rose sixfold between January 1991 and February 1992.

Relations with the C.I.S. and Europe

The Baltic states are still economically tied to the former Soviet states, most of which have formed a Commonwealth of Independent States, known as the C.I.S.

The pollution caused by this oil-shale plant at Kohtla-Jarve will be expensive to clean up.

The Baltic states may have gained their independence, but they may suffer economically. Indeed, living standards in the Baltic states have fallen. In 1992, the new Estonian prime minister, Tiit Vahi, announced that putting industry and commerce into private hands must take second place to making sure there was enough food and heating.

Co-operation

The Baltic states will have to co-operate to build up their economies during the next few years. They will probably resume their role as an essential economic link between Western and Eastern Europe. They may also play an important part in any future central European trading bloc, including the former Soviet satellites in Eastern Europe. Too great an economic dependence on either Western Europe or the C.I.S. could bring new problems. However, it is likely that the Baltic peoples have the ability and the resources to overcome the economic obstacles which lie in their path.

Collective farming of cattle in Estonia

Agricultural exports are important economically.

FACTS AND FIGURES

Lithuania
Area: 64,750 sq km (25,000 sq miles).
Capital: Vilnius.
Population: 3.7 million (1989).
Elevation: Highest – Juozapines, 292 m (958 ft). Lowest – sea level along the coast.
Major Rivers: Neman, Neris, Nevezys.
Climate: A moderate continental climate, with cold winters, and warm, wet summers.
Vegetation: Forests covering about 25% of the land, of which approximately 38% are pine and the remainder broadleaf.
Wildlife: Bears and wolves in the forests.
Agriculture: Dairy products, beef cattle, potatoes, flax.
Industry: Shipyards, metalwork, machinery manufacture, oil refining, chemical production.
Ethnic Mix: Lithuanians 80%, Russians 9%, Poles 7%, Belarussians 1.7%, Ukrainians 1.2%.
Language: Lithuanian.
Religion: Christianity is the dominant religion.

Latvia
Area: 63,710 sq km (24,600 sq miles).
Capital: Riga.
Population: 2.7 million (1989).
Elevation: Highest – Gaizins Mt, 311 m (1,020 ft.). Lowest – sea level.
Major Rivers: Daugava (Western Dvina), Gauja, Venta.
Climate: Long cold winters, cool, wet summers.
Vegetation: Swamp and forest covers 40% of the land. The remainder is rolling pasture.
Wildlife: Bears, wolves, and elk live in the forests of the region.
Agriculture: Dairy products, beef cattle, barley, oats, potatoes, flax.
Industry: Electronics, heavy machinery

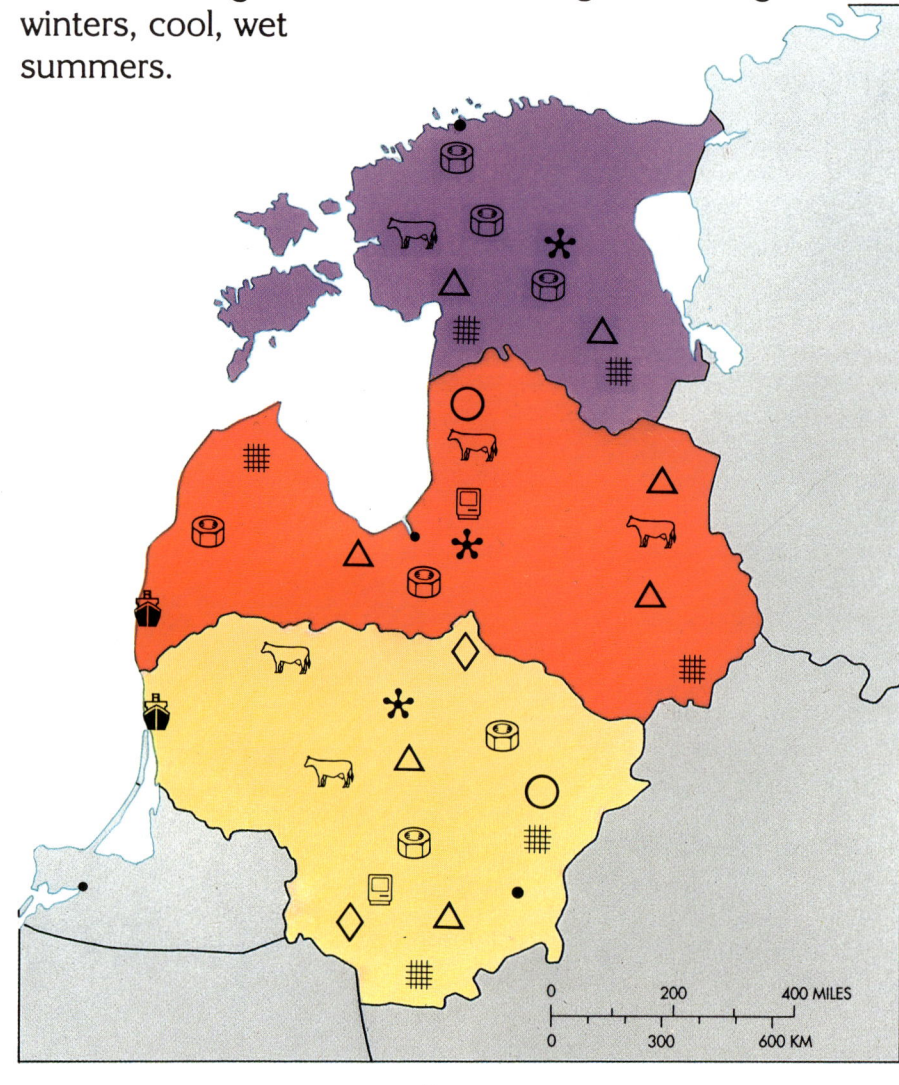

- Dairying
- Machinery
- Sugar Beets
- Textiles
- Potatoes
- Shipyard
- Flax
- Peat
- Electronics

28

manufacture, building materials, steel mills, forestry, processed foods, fishing.
Ethnic Mix: Latvians 51%, Russians 34%, Belarussians 4.5%, Ukrainians 3.5%, Poles 2.3%.
Language: Latvian.
Religion: Christianity.

Estonia
Area: 45,066 sq km (17,400 sq miles).
Capital: Tallinn.
Population: 1.6 million (1992).
Elevation: Highest – Munamagi, 318 m (1,043 ft). Lowest – sea level along the coast.
Major Rivers are the Ema, Narva and Parnu.
Climate: Transitional between maritime and continental, with sea winds preventing extremes of temperature.
Vegetation: Swamp and forest (broadleaf and conifer) cover about 30% of the country. The remainder is low-lying farmland.
Wildlife: Game of all kinds live in the forests, including wild boar, lynx, bears, and elk. Ringed seal and grey seal off the coast.
Agriculture: Dairy products, barley, chickens, pigs, beef cattle, rye and potatoes are the main agricultural exports.
Industry: Hydro-electric power, oil-shale, oil refining, chemicals, heavy machinery manufacture, processed foods, textiles, fashion and design in Tallinn.
Ethnic Mix: Estonians 61.5%, Russians 30.3 %, Ukrainians 3.1 %, Belarussians 1.8 %.
Language: Estonian.
Religion: Christianity.

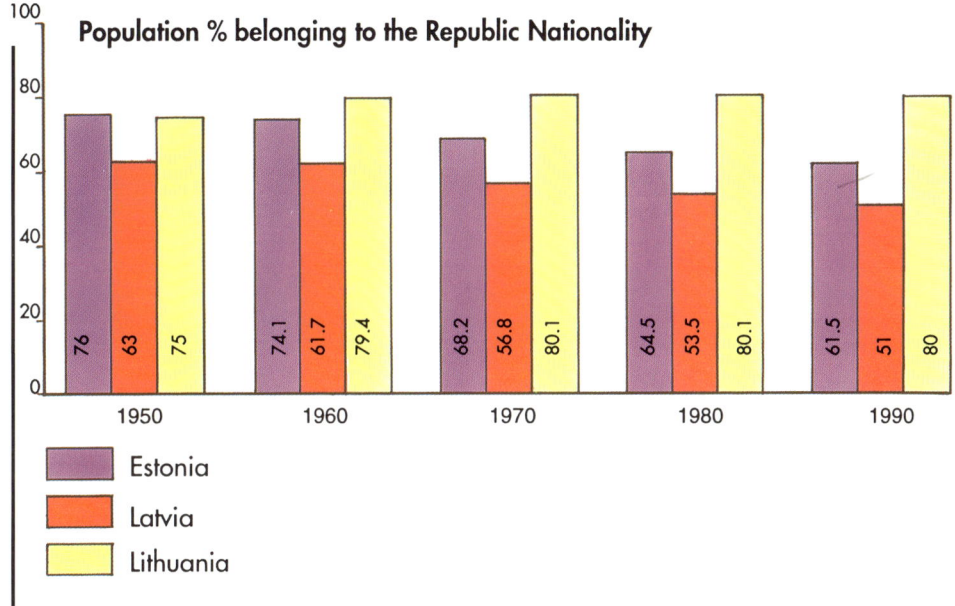

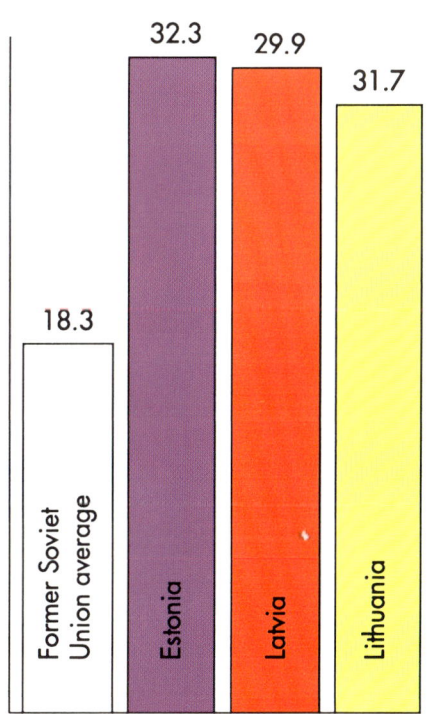
Grain harvest (centners per ha, 1987)

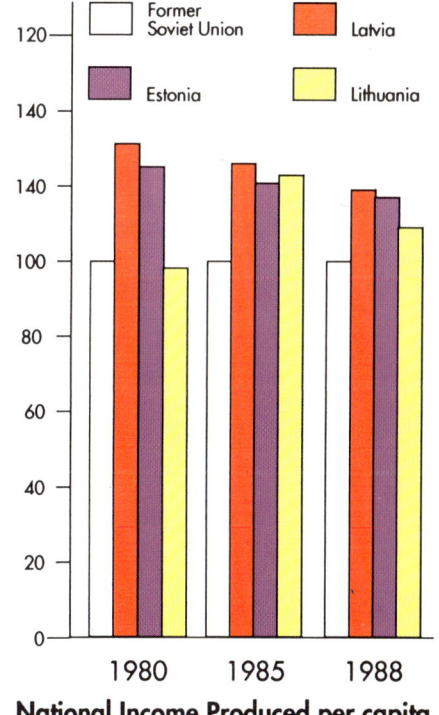
National Income Produced per capita

29

CHRONOLOGY AND FAMOUS PEOPLE

c. 3000 B.C. Tribal ancestors of modern Lithuanians, Latvians, and Estonians establish themselves in the Baltic lands
c. A.D. 650 Viking raids begin several hundred years of trading and fighting between Scandinavians and Baltic tribes
1201 Foundation of the city of Riga, centre of commercial life in the military state of Livonia
1236 The Lithuanian tribes unite under Mindaugas
1346 The Danish monarchy sells its rights to Estonia to the Teutonic Order
1386 The Lithuanian prince Jagiello marries the Polish heiress Jadwiga and orders the mass baptism of his subjects
1410 Defeat of the Teutonic Knights at Tannenberg
1569 Formal union of Lithuania and Poland
1795 Lithuania follows Latvia and Estonia into the Russian Empire

Adolf Hitler (1889-1945) He became dictator of Germany in 1933. From 1941 to 1944, the Baltic states became part of his Nazi Empire. Hitler almost wiped out the Jewish population of the Baltics during World War II.

1811 Emancipation of the serfs in Estonia
1830 Lithuanian nobility and peasants join the Polish uprising against Russia
1861 Emancipation of the serfs in Lithuania
1863 Lithuanian nobility and peasants join second Polish uprising against the Tsar
1905 General strike in the Baltic provinces, and violence against the Baltic-Germans, accompany the revolutionary upheavals in the Russian Empire
1914 Outbreak of World War I
1915 Lithuania occupied by German troops
1917 Revolutions in Russia: the communists seize power
1918 Lithuania declares its independence on February 16, followed by Estonia (February 24), and Latvia (November 18)
1939 The Nazi-Soviet pact between Germany and the Soviet Union states that the Baltics are part of the Soviet sphere of influence
1940 The Red Army occupies the Baltic states and they are absorbed

Joseph Stalin (1879-1953) Stalin emerged as the dictator of the Soviet Union in 1928. His Red Army occupied the Baltic states in 1940, following the Nazi-Soviet pact of 1939. He ordered thousands of deportations.

Mikhail Gorbachev (1931-) He attempted to bring political and economic reform in the Soviet Union, providing the Baltic republics with the weapon with which to fight for their independence.

into the Soviet Union
1941 Nazi Germany invades the Soviet Union and rapidly overruns the Baltic republics
1944 The Red Army returns to the Baltic States
1952 End of the guerrilla resistance to the Soviet Union in the republics
1972 Student and worker protests against Soviet rule. Romas Kalanta burns himself to death in protest and others follow his example
1985 Mikhail Gorbachev comes to power in the Soviet Union

1986-87 Mass demonstrations in the Baltic republics against environmental destruction by Soviet industry and armed forces
1988 Founding of the Popular Fronts in the Baltic states
1989 Human chain stretching across the republics is formed on 23 August, to mark the fiftieth anniversary of the Nazi-Soviet pact. In December, the Lithuanian Communist Party separates from the Soviet Party. Mikhail Gorbachev

Vytautas Landsbergis (1932-) A Lithuanian music professor who played a leading role in his country's struggle for independence. He became president of Lithuania when it declared its independence from the Soviet Union.

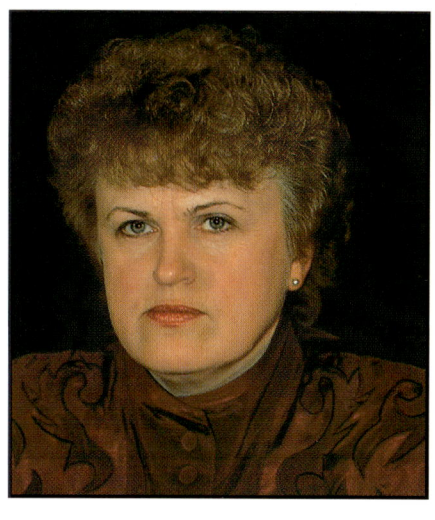

Kazimiera Prunskiene (1943-) A professor of economics at Vilnius University from 1965 to 1985, she became prime minister of a newly independent Lithuania in 1990. She was forced to resign in 1991.

visits Lithuania.
1990 On 11 March, Lithuanian parliament votes to restore Lithuanian independence. Latvia follows on 30 March, and Estonia on 4 May. In April the Soviet Union imposes an economic blockade on Lithuania
1991 February, violence flares in Lithuania and Latvia. August, Mikhail Gorbachev survives a coup. On 6 September, the Soviet Union recognises Lithuanian, Latvian and Estonian independence

INDEX

Aestii people 10
agriculture 7, 18-19, 28, 29

Baltic tribes 10
Baltic-German rulers 6, 11, 14, 15
Belarus 12, 26
borders 15
Brothers of the Sword 11, 12

Christianity 11, 14
citizenship 9, 24
climate 9, 28, 29
Commonwealth of Independent States (C.I.S.) 4, 9, 26, 27
communism 7, 16, 21
currency 26

democratic government 16, 17
deportations 19

economic partnerships 25, 27
economic problems 6-7, 24, 26-7
economy 16-17, 18-19
energy resources 8, 9, 26
environmental problems 7, 9, 19
Estland 11
Estonia 6, 8, 9, 10, 11, 13, 14, 15, 16, 17, 18, 19, 21, 22, 23, 24, 29
ethnic mix 28, 29
European Community (E.C.) 25

Forest Brothers 18
free enterprise 7

geography 8, 28, 29
German colonisation 11

German military orders 11, 12, 13
Germany 15, 16, 17, 18, 25
glasnost 21
Gorbachev, Mikhail 21, 23, 31

Hitler, Adolf 30

independence 16, 21, 22, 23
industrial pollution 7, 9, 21
industrialisation programme, Soviet 6, 19
industry and commerce 7, 9, 28, 29
international relations 25

Jewish persecution 18

land reform 16
Landsbergis, Vytautas 6, 31
language 9, 13, 14, 15, 19, 22, 28, 29
Latvia 6, 8, 9, 11, 13, 14, 15, 16, 17, 18, 19, 20, 22, 23, 28-9
Lithuania 6, 8, 9, 12-13, 14, 15, 16, 17, 18, 19, 22-3, 24, 26, 28
living standards 20, 27
Livonia 10, 11, 13

Mindaugas 12
minorities 6, 9, 19, 22, 24

nationalism 15, 21
natural resources 8, 26
Nazi-Soviet Pact 17, 22
Nazis 18

paganism 10, 12
perestroika 21
Poland 12-13, 14, 17

Polish-Lithuanian alliance 13
Popular Fronts 21, 22, 23
populations 9, 28, 29
Prunskiene, Kazimiera 31
Prussia 13

Red Army 16, 17, 18
religion 6, 10-11, 14, 28, 29
resistance movements 18
Riga 11, 14, 20, 23
Russia 11, 13, 14, 15, 16
Russian Federation 24
Russian immigrants 6, 9, 19, 20, 22, 24
Russification policy 14, 15

Savissar, Edgar 24
Scandinavia 20, 25
Smetona, Antanas 17
Soviet Union 4, 6-7, 9, 16, 17-19, 20, 21, 23, 24, 25, 26
Stalin, Joseph 30
Sweden 11, 13

Tacitus 10
Tallinn 11, 20
Teutonic Knights 11, 12, 13
trade 10, 11, 17
trading blocs 25, 27
troop withdrawals 24

Vagnorius, Gediminas 24
Vahi, Tiit 27
Vikings 10
Vilnius 6, 16, 23

World War I 15
World War II 17-18

Yeltsin, Boris 21

PHOTOCREDITS

Cover and pages 6, 9, 10 bottom right, 19, 20, 22-23 all, 24, 25, 31 top right and bottom: Frank Spooner Pictures: 6-7, 7, 8, 10 bottom left, 12, 13, 16 top, 17, 18, 18-19, 21, 26, 27 both, 30 bottom and 31 top left; Novosti RIA; 10 top, 11, 14 and 30 top: Mary Evans Picture Library; 16 bottom: Popperfoto.